The Lays
of Ancient Rome

DEATH OF SEXTUS

The Lays of Ancient Rome

By

Thomas Babington Macaulay

Illustrated by

Norman Ault

London

Williams & Norgate

14 Henrietta Street, Covent Garden

1911

CONTENTS

LIST OF COLOURED PLATES

HORATIUS

A LAY MADE ABOUT THE YEAR OF
THE CITY CCCLX

I

Lars Porsena of Clusium
  By the Nine Gods he swore
That the great house of Tarquin
  Should suffer wrong no more.
By the Nine Gods he swore it,
  And named a trysting day,

And bade his messengers ride forth,
East and west and south and north,
  To summon his array.

II

East and west and south and north
  The messengers ride fast,
And tower and town and cottage
  Have heard the trumpet's blast.
Shame on the false Etruscan
  Who lingers in his home,
When Porsena of Clusium
  Is on the march for Rome.

III

The horsemen and the footmen
  Are pouring in amain,
From many a stately market-place ;
  From many a fruitful plain ;

From many a lonely hamlet,
    Which, hid by beech and pine,
Like an eagle's nest, hangs on the crest
    Of purple Apennine ;

IV

From lordly Volaterræ,
    Where scowls the far-famed hold
Piled by the hands of giants
    For godlike kings of old ;
From seagirt Populonia,
    Whose sentinels descry
Sardinia's snowy mountain-tops
    Fringing the southern sky ;

V

From the proud mart of Pisæ,
    Queen of the western waves,

Where ride Massilia's triremes
    Heavy with fair-haired slaves ;
From where sweet Clanis wanders
    Through corn and vines and flowers ;
From where Cortona lifts to heaven
    Her diadem of towers.

VI

Tall are the oaks whose acorns
    Drop in dark Auser's rill ;
Fat are the stags that champ the boughs
    Of the Ciminian hill ;
Beyond all streams Clitumnus
    Is to the herdsman dear ;
Best of all pools the fowler loves
    The great Volsinian mere.

VII

But now no stroke of woodman
    Is heard by Auser's rill ;

THE VATS OF LUNA

No hunter tracks the stag's green path
   Up the Ciminian hill ;
Unwatched along Clitumnus
   Grazes the milk-white steer ;
Unharmed the water fowl may dip
   In the Volsinian mere.

VIII

The harvests of Arretium,
   This year, old men shall reap ;
This year, young boys in Umbro
   Shall plunge the struggling sheep ;
And in the vats of Luna,
   This year, the must shall foam
Round the white feet of laughing girls
   Whose sires have marched to Rome.

IX

There be thirty chosen prophets,
   The wisest of the land,

Who alway by Lars Porsena
    Both morn and evening stand :
Evening and morn the Thirty
    Have turned the verses o'er,
Traced from the right on linen white
    By mighty seers of yore.

X

And with one voice the Thirty
    Have their glad answer given :
" Go forth, go forth, Lars Porsena ;
    Go forth, beloved of Heaven ;
Go, and return in glory
    To Clusium's royal dome ;
And hang round Nurscia's altars
    The golden shields of Rome."

XI

And now hath every city
    Sent up her tale of men ;

The foot are fourscore thousand,
  The horse are thousands ten.
Before the gates of Sutrium
  Is met the great array.
A proud man was Lars Porsena
  Upon the trysting day.

XII

For all the Etruscan armies
  Were ranged beneath his eye,
And many a banished Roman,
  And many a stout ally ;
And with a mighty following
  To join the muster came
The Tusculan Mamilius,
  Prince of the Latian name.

XIII

But by the yellow Tiber
  Was tumult and affright :

From all the spacious champaign
  To Rome men took their flight.
A mile around the city,
  The throng stopped up the ways ;
A fearful sight it was to see
  Through two long nights and days.

XIV

For aged folks on crutches,
  And women great with child,
And mothers sobbing over babes
  That clung to them and smiled,
And sick men borne in litters
  High on the necks of slaves,
And troops of sun-burned husbandmen
  With reaping-hooks and staves,

XV

And droves of mules and asses
  Laden with skins of wine,

And endless flocks of goats and sheep,
  And endless herds of kine,
And endless trains of waggons
  That creaked beneath the weight
Of corn-sacks and of household goods,
  Choked every roaring gate.

XVI

Now, from the rock Tarpeian,
  Could the wan burghers spy
The line of blazing villages
  Red in the midnight sky.
The Fathers of the City,
  They sat all night and day,
For every hour some horseman came
  With tidings of dismay.

XVII

To eastward and to westward
  Have spread the Tuscan bands ;

Nor house, nor fence, nor dovecot
In Crustumerium stands.
Verbenna down to Ostia
Hath wasted all the plain ;
Astur hath stormed Janiculum,
And the stout guards are slain.

XVIII

I wis, in all the Senate,
There was no heart so bold,
But sore it ached, and fast it beat,
When that ill news was told.
Forthwith up rose the Consul,
Up rose the Fathers all ;
In haste they girded up their gowns,
And hied them to the wall.

XIX

They held a council standing
Before the River-Gate ;

Short time was there, ye well may guess,
    For musing or debate.
Out spake the Consul roundly :
    " The bridge must straight go down;
For, since Janiculum is lost,
    Nought else can save the town."

XX

Just then a scout came flying,
    All wild with haste and fear :
" To arms ! to arms ! Sir Consul :
    Lars Porsena is here."
On the low hills to westward
    The Consul fixed his eye,
And saw the swarthy storm of dust
    Rise fast along the sky.

XXI

And nearer fast and nearer
    Doth the red whirlwind come ;

And louder still and still more loud,
From underneath that rolling cloud,
Is heard the trumpet's war-note proud,
    The trampling, and the hum.
And plainly and more plainly
    Now through the gloom appears,
Far to left and far to right,
In broken gleams of dark-blue light,
The long array of helmets bright,
    The long array of spears.

XXII

And plainly and more plainly,
    Above that glimmering line,
Now might ye see the banners
    Of twelve fair cities shine ;
But the banner of proud Clusium
    Was highest of them all,

The terror of the Umbrian,
   The terror of the Gaul.

XXIII

And plainly and more plainly
   Now might the burghers know,
By port and vest, by horse and crest,
   Each warlike Lucumo.
There Cilnius of Arretium
   On his fleet roan was seen ;
And Astur of the four-fold shield,
Girt with the brand none else may wield,
Tolumnius with the belt of gold,
And dark Verbenna from the hold
   By reedy Thrasymene.

XXIV

Fast by the royal standard,
   O'erlooking all the war,

Lars Porsena of Clusium
   Sat in his ivory car.
By the right wheel rode Mamilius,
   Prince of the Latian name ;
And by the left false Sextus,
   That wrought the deed of shame.

XXV

But when the face of Sextus
   Was seen among the foes,
A yell that rent the firmament
   From all the town arose.
On the house-tops was no woman
   But spat towards him and hissed,
No child but screamed out curses,
   And shook its little fist.

XXVI

But the Consul's brow was sad,
   And the Consul's speech was low,

And darkly looked he at the wall,
   And darkly at the foe.
" Their van will be upon us
   Before the bridge goes down ;
And if they once may win the bridge,
   What hope to save the town ? "

XXVII

Then out spake brave Horatius,
   The Captain of the Gate :
" To every man upon this earth
   Death cometh soon or late.
And how can man die better
   Than facing fearful odds,
For the ashes of his fathers,
   And the temples of his Gods,

XXVIII

" And for the tender mother
   Who dandled him to rest,

And for the wife who nurses
    His baby at her breast,
And for the holy maidens
    Who feed the eternal flame,
To save them from false Sextus
    That wrought the deed of shame ?

XXIX

" Hew down the bridge, Sir Consul,
    With all the speed ye may ;
I, with two more to help me,
    Will hold the foe in play.
In yon strait path a thousand
    May well be stopped by three.
Now who will stand on either hand,
    And keep the bridge with me ? "

XXX

Then out spake Spurius Lartius ;
    A Ramnian proud was he :

"Lo, I will stand at thy right hand,
  And keep the bridge with thee."
And out spake strong Herminius;
  Of Titian blood was he:
"I will abide on thy left side,
  And keep the bridge with thee."

XXXI

"Horatius," quoth the Consul,
  "As thou sayest, so let it be."
And straight against that great array
  Forth went the dauntless Three.
For Romans in Rome's quarrel
  Spared neither land nor gold,
Nor son nor wife, nor limb nor life,
  In the brave days of old.

XXXII

Then none was for a party;
  Then all were for the state;

2

Then the great man helped the poor,
 And the poor man loved the great :
Then lands were fairly portioned ;
 Then spoils were fairly sold :
The Romans were like brothers
 In the brave days of old.

XXXIII

Now Roman is to Roman
 More hateful than a foe,
And the Tribunes beard the high,
 And the Fathers grind the low.
As we wax hot in faction,
 In battle we wax cold :
Wherefore men fight not as they fought
 In the brave days of old.

XXXIV

Now while the Three were tightening
 Their harness on their backs,

The Consul was the foremost man
   To take in hand an axe :
And Fathers mixed with Commons,
   Seized hatchet, bar, and crow,
And smote upon the planks above,
   And loosed the props below.

XXXV

Meanwhile the Tuscan army,
   Right glorious to behold,
Came flashing back the noonday light,
Rank behind rank, like surges bright,
   Of a broad sea of gold.
Four hundred trumpets sounded
   A peal of warlike glee,
As that great host, with measured tread,
And spears advanced, and ensigns spread,
Rolled slowly towards the bridge's head,
   Where stood the dauntless Three.

XXXVI

The Three stood calm and silent,
    And looked upon the foes,
And a great shout of laughter
    From all the vanguard rose :
And forth three chiefs came spurring
    Before that deep array ;
To earth they sprang, their swords they
      drew,
And lifted high their shields, and flew
    To win the narrow way ;

XXXVII

Aunus from green Tifernum,
    Lord of the Hill of Vines ;
And Seius, whose eight hundred slaves
    Sicken in Ilva's mines ;
And Picus, long to Clusium
    Vassal in peace and war,

Who led to fight his Umbrian powers
From that grey crag where, girt with
    towers,
The fortress of Nequinum lowers
   O'er the pale waves of Nar.

XXXVIII

Stout Lartius hurled down Aunus
   Into the stream beneath :
Herminius struck at Seius,
   And clove him to the teeth :
At Picus brave Horatius
   Darted one fiery thrust ;
And the proud Umbrian's gilded arms
   Clashed in the bloody dust.

XXXIX

Then Ocnus of Falerii
   Rushed on the Roman Three,

And Lausulus of Urgo,
    The rover of the sea ;
And Aruns of Volsinium,
    Who slew the great wild boar,
The great wild boar that had his den
Amidst the reeds of Cosa's fen,
And wasted fields, and slaughtered men,
    Along Albinia's shore.

XL

Herminius smote down Aruns :
    Lartius laid Ocnus low :
Right to the heart of Lausulus
    Horatius sent a blow.
" Lie there," he cried, " fell pirate !
    No more, aghast and pale,
From Ostia's walls the crowd shall mark
The track of thy destroying bark ;

No more Campania's hinds shall fly
To woods and caverns when they spy
   Thy thrice accursed sail."

XLI

But now no sound of laughter
   Was heard among the foes.
A wild and wrathful clamour
   From all the vanguard rose.
Six spears' lengths from the entrance
   Halted that deep array,
And for a space no man came forth
   To win the narrow way.

XLII

But hark ! the cry is Astur :
   And lo ! the ranks divide ;
And the great Lord of Luna
   Comes with his stately stride.

Upon his ample shoulders
　　Clangs loud the four-fold shield,
And in his hand he shakes the brand
　　Which none but he can wield.

XLIII

He smiled on those bold Romans
　　A smile serene and high ;
He eyed the flinching Tuscans,
　　And scorn was in his eye.
Quoth he, " The she-wolf's litter
　　Stand savagely at bay :
But will you dare to follow,
　　If Astur clears the way ? "

XLIV

Then, whirling up his broadsword
　　With both hands to the height,

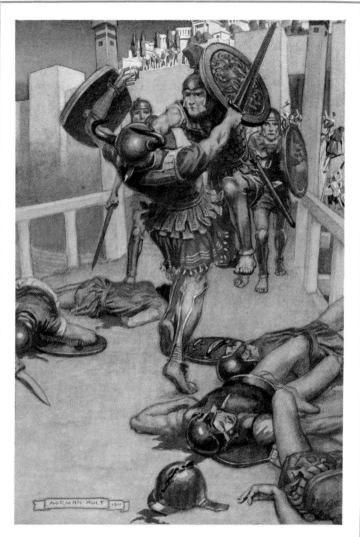

DEATH OF ASTUR

He rushed against Horatius,
    And smote with all his might.
With shield and blade Horatius
    Right deftly turned the blow.
The blow, though turned, came yet too
      nigh ;
It missed his helm, but gashed his thigh :
The Tuscans raised a joyful cry
    To see the red blood flow.

XLV

He reeled, and on Herminius
    He leaned one breathing-space ;
Then, like a wild cat mad with wounds,
    Sprang right at Astur's face.
Through teeth, and skull, and helmet
    So fierce a thrust he sped,
The good sword stood a hand-breadth out
    Behind the Tuscan's head.

XLVI

And the great Lord of Luna
    Fell at that deadly stroke,
As falls on Mount Alvernus
    A thunder-smitten oak.
Far o'er the crashing forest
    The giant arms lie spread ;
And the pale augurs, muttering low,
    Gaze on the blasted head.

XLVII

On Astur's throat Horatius
    Right firmly pressed his heel,
And thrice and four times tugged amain,
    Ere he wrenched out the steel.
" And see," he cried, " the welcome,
    Fair guests, that waits you here !
What noble Lucumo comes next
    To taste our Roman cheer ? "

XLVIII

But at his haughty challenge
  A sullen murmur ran,
Mingled of wrath, and shame, and dread,
  Along that glittering van.
There lacked not men of prowess,
  Nor men of lordly race ;
For all Etruria's noblest
  Were round the fatal place.

XLIX

But all Etruria's noblest
  Felt their hearts sink to see
On the earth the bloody corpses,
  In the path the dauntless Three :
And, from the ghastly entrance
  Where those bold Romans stood,
All shrank, like boys who unaware,

Ranging the woods to start a hare,
Come to the mouth of the dark lair
Where, growling low, a fierce old bear
    Lies amidst bones and blood.

L

Was none who would be foremost
    To lead such dire attack :
But those behind cried " Forward ! "
    And those before cried " Back ! "
And backward now and forward
    Wavers the deep array ;
And on the tossing sea of steel,
To and fro the standards reel ;
And the victorious trumpet-peal
    Dies fitfully away.

LI

Yet one man for one moment
    Strode out before the crowd ;

Well known was he to all the Three,
　　And they gave him greeting loud.
" Now welcome, welcome, Sextus !
　　Now welcome to thy home !
Why dost thou stay, and turn away ?
　　Here lies the road to Rome."

LII

Thrice looked he at the city ;
　　Thrice looked he at the dead ;
And thrice came on in fury,
　　And thrice turned back in dread :
And, white with fear and hatred,
　　Scowled at the narrow way
Where, wallowing in a pool of blood,
　　The bravest Tuscans lay.

LIII

But meanwhile axe and lever
　　Have manfully been plied ;

And now the bridge hangs tottering
  Above the boiling tide.
" Come back, come back, Horatius ! "
  Loud cried the Fathers all.
" Back, Lartius ! back Herminius !
  Back, ere the ruin fall ! "

LIV

Back darted Spurius Lartius ;
  Herminius darted back :
And, as they passed, beneath their feet
  They felt the timbers crack.
But when they turned their faces,
  And on the farther shore
Saw brave Horatius stand alone,
  They would have crossed once more.

LV

But with a crash like thunder
  Fell every loosen'd beam,

HORATIUS

And, like a dam, the mighty wreck
  Lay right athwart the stream :
And a long shout of triumph
  Rose from the walls of Rome,
As to the highest turret-tops
  Was splashed the yellow foam.

LVI

And, like a horse unbroken
  When first he feels the rein,
The furious river struggled hard,
  And tossed his tawny mane,
And burst the curb, and bounded,
  Rejoicing to be free,
And whirling down, in fierce career,
Battlement, and plank, and pier,
  Rushed headlong to the sea.

LVII

Alone stood brave Horatius,
　　But constant still in mind ;
Thrice thirty thousand foes before,
　　And the broad flood behind.
" Down with him ! " cried false Sextus,
　　With a smile on his pale face.
" Now yield thee," cried Lars Porsena,
　　" Now yield thee to our grace."

LVIII

Round turned he, as not deigning
　　Those craven ranks to see ;
Nought spake he to Lars Porsena,
　　To Sextus nought spake he ;
But he saw on Palatinus
　　The white porch of his home ;
And he spake to the noble river
　　That rolls by the towers of Rome.

LIX

" Oh, Tiber ! father Tiber !
   To whom the Romans pray,
A Roman's life, a Roman's arms,
   Take thou in charge this day ! "
So he spake, and speaking sheathed
   The good sword by his side,
And with his harness on his back,
   Plunged headlong in the tide.

LX

No sound of joy or sorrow
   Was heard from either bank ;
But friends and foes in dumb surprise,
With parted lips and straining eyes,
   Stood gazing where he sank ;
And when above the surges
   They saw his crest appear,

3

All Rome sent forth a rapturous cry,
And even the ranks of Tuscany
  Could scarce forbear to cheer.

LXI

But fiercely ran the current,
  Swollen high by months of rain :
And fast his blood was flowing ;
  And he was sore in pain,
And heavy with his armour,
  And spent with changing blows :
And oft they thought him sinking,
  But still again he rose.

LXII

Never, I ween, did swimmer,
  In such an evil case,
Struggle through such a raging flood
Safe to the landing place :

But his limbs were borne up bravely
   By the brave heart within,
And our good father Tiber
   Bare bravely up his chin.

LXIII

" Curse on him ! " quoth false Sextus ;
   " Will not the villain drown ?
But for this stay, ere close of day
   We should have sacked the town ! "
" Heaven help him ! " quoth Lars Porsena,
   " And bring him safe to shore ;
For such a gallant feat of arms
   Was never seen before."

LXIV

And now he feels the bottom ;
   Now on dry earth he stands ;
Now round him throng the Fathers
   To press his gory hands ;

And now, with shouts and clapping,
    And noise of weeping loud,
He enters through the River-Gate,
    Borne by the joyous crowd.

LXV

They gave him of the corn-land,
    That was of public right,
As much as two strong oxen
    Could plough from morn till night ;
And they made a molten image,
    And set it up on high,
And there it stands unto this day
    To witness if I lie.

LXVI

It stands in the Comitium,
    Plain for all folks to see ;

Horatius in his harness,
    Halting upon one knee :
And underneath is written,
    In letters all of gold,
How valiantly he kept the bridge
    In the brave days of old.

LXVII

And still his name sounds stirring
    Unto the men of Rome,
As the trumpet-blast that cries to them
    To charge the Volscian home ;
And wives still pray to Juno
    For boys with hearts as bold
As his who kept the bridge so well
    In the brave days of old.

LXVIII

And in the nights of winter,
    When the cold north winds blow,

And the long howling of the wolves
　　Is heard amidst the snow ;
When round the lonely cottage
　　Roars loud the tempest's din,
And the good logs of Algidus
　　Roar louder yet within ;

LXIX

When the oldest cask is opened,
　　And the largest lamp is lit ;
When the chestnuts glow in the embers,
　　And the kid turns on the spit ;
When young and old in circle
　　Around the firebrands close ;
When the girls are weaving baskets,
　　And the lads are shaping bows ;

LXX

When the goodman mends his armour,
　　And trims his helmet's plume ;

When the goodwife's shuttle merrily
　Goes flashing through the loom ;
With weeping and with laughter
　Still is the story told,
How well Horatius kept the bridge
　In the brave days of old.

THE BATTLE OF THE LAKE REGILLUS

A LAY SUNG AT THE FEAST OF CASTOR AND POLLUX ON THE IDES OF QUINTILIS, IN THE YEAR OF THE CITY CCCCLI

I

Ho, trumpets, sound a war-note !
Ho, lictors, clear the way !
The Knights will ride, in all their pride,
Along the streets to-day.

To-day the doors and windows
  Are hung with garlands all,
From Castor in the Forum,
  To Mars without the wall.
Each Knight is robed in purple,
  With olive each is crowned ;
A gallant war-horse under each
  Paws haughtily the ground.
While flows the Yellow River,
  While stands the Sacred Hill,
The proud Ides of Quintilis
  Shall have such honour still.
Gay are the Martian Kalends :
  December's Nones are gay :
But the proud Ides, when the squadron
    rides,
  Shall be Rome's whitest day.

THE GREAT TWIN BRETHREN

II

Unto the Great Twin Brethren
    We keep this solemn feast.
Swift, swift, the Great Twin Brethren
    Came spurring from the east.
They came o'er wild Parthenius
    Tossing in waves of pine,
O'er Cirrha's dome, o'er Adria's foam,
    O'er purple Apennine,
From where with flutes and dances
    Their ancient mansion rings,
In lordly Lacedæmon,
    The City of two kings,
To where, by Lake Regillus,
    Under the Porcian height,
All in the lands of Tusculum,
    Was fought the glorious fight.

III

Now on the place of slaughter
    Are cots and sheepfolds seen,
And rows of vines, and fields of wheat,
    And apple-orchards green !
The swine crush the big acorns
    That fall from Corne's oaks.
Upon the turf by the Fair Fount
    The reaper's pottage smokes.
The fisher baits his angle ;
    The hunter twangs his bow ;
Little they think on those strong limbs
    That moulder deep below.
Little they think how sternly
    That day the trumpets pealed ;
How in the slippery swamp of blood
    Warrior and war-horse reeled ;

How wolves came with fierce gallop,
   And crows on eager wings,
To tear the flesh of captains,
   And peck the eyes of kings ;
How thick the dead lay scattered
   Under the Porcian height ;
How through the gates of Tusculum
   Raved the wild stream of flight ;
And how the Lake Regillus
   Bubbled with crimson foam,
What time the Thirty Cities
   Came forth to war with Rome.

IV

But, Roman, when thou standest
   Upon that holy ground,
Look thou with heed on the dark rock
   That girds the dark lake round.

So shalt thou see a hoof-mark
  Stamped deep into the flint :
It was no hoof of mortal steed
  That made so strange a dint :
There to the Great Twin Brethren
  Vow thou thy vows, and pray
That they, in tempest and in fight,
  Will keep thy head alway.

V

Since last the Great Twin Brethren
  Of mortal eyes were seen,
Have years gone by an hundred
  And fourscore and thirteen.
That summer a Virginius
  Was Consul first in place ;
The second was stout Aulus,
  Of the Posthumian race.

The Herald of the Latines
   From Gabii came in state :
The Herald of the Latines
   Passed through Rome's Eastern Gate :
The Herald of the Latines
   Did in our Forum stand ;
And there he did his office,
   A sceptre in his hand.

VI

" Hear, Senators and people
   Of the good town of Rome :
The Thirty Cities charge you
   To bring the Tarquins home :
And if ye still be stubborn,
   To work the Tarquins wrong,
The Thirty Cities warn you,
   Look that your walls be strong."

VII

Then spake the Consul Aulus,
    He spake a bitter jest :
" Once the jays sent a message
    Unto the eagle's nest : —
Now yield thou up thine eyrie
    Unto the carrion-kite,
Or come forth valiantly, and face
    The jays in deadly fight.—
Forth looked in wrath the eagle ;
    And carrion-kite and jay,
Soon as they saw his beak and claw,
    Fled screaming far away."

VIII

The Herald of the Latines
    Hath hied him back in state :
The Fathers of the City
    Are met in high debate.

Then spake the elder Consul,
　　An ancient man and wise :
" Now hearken, Conscript Fathers,
　　To that which I advise.
In seasons of great peril
　　'Tis good that one bear sway ;
Then choose we a Dictator,
　　Whom all men shall obey.
Camerium knows how deeply
　　The sword of Aulus bites ;
And all our City calls him
　　The man of seventy fights.
Then let him be Dictator
　　For six months and no more,
And have a Master of the Knights,
　　And axes twenty-four."

4

IX

So Aulus was Dictator,
     The man of seventy fights ;
He made Æbutius Elva
     His Master of the Knights.
On the third morn thereafter,
     At dawning of the day,
Did Aulus and Æbutius
     Set forth with their array.
Sempronius Atratinus
     Was left in charge at home
With   boys,   and   with   grey-headed
          men,
     To keep the walls of Rome.
Hard by the Lake Regillus
     Our camp was pitched at night :
Eastward a mile the Latines lay,
     Under the Porcian height.

Far over hill and valley
  Their mighty host was spread ;
And with their thousand watch-fires
  The midnight sky was red.

                    X

Up rose the golden morning
  Over the Porcian height,
The proud Ides of Quintilis
  Marked evermore with white.
Nor without secret trouble
  Our bravest saw the foes ;
For girt by threescore thousand spears,
  The thirty standards rose.
From every warlike city
  That boasts the Latian name,
Foredoomed to dogs and vultures,
  That gallant army came ;

From Setia's purple vineyards,
   From Norba's ancient wall,
From the white streets of Tusculum,
   The proudest town of all ;
From where the Witch's Fortress
   O'erhangs the dark-blue seas ;
From the still glassy lake that sleeps
   Beneath Aricia's trees—
Those trees in whose dim shadow
   The ghastly priest doth reign,
The priest who slew the slayer,
   And shall himself be slain ;
From the drear banks of Ufens,
   Where flights of marsh-fowl play,
And buffaloes lie wallowing
   Through the hot summer's day ;
From the gigantic watch-towers,
   No work of earthly men,

Whence Cora's sentinels o'erlook
   The never-ending fen ;
From the Laurentian jungle,
   The wild hog's reedy home ;
From the green steeps whence Anio leaps
   In floods of snow-white foam.

XI

Aricia, Cora, Norba,
   Velitræ, with the might
Of Setia and of Tusculum,
   Were marshalled on the right :
The leader was Mamilius,
   Prince of the Latian name ;
Upon his head a helmet
   Of red gold shone like flame :
High on a gallant charger
   Of dark-grey hue he rode ;

Over his gilded armour
    A vest of purple flowed,
Woven in the land of sunrise
    By Syria's dark-browed daughters,
And by the sails of Carthage brought
    Far o'er the southern waters.

XII

Lavinium and Laurentum
    Had on the left their post,
With all the banners of the marsh,
    And banners of the coast.
Their leader was false Sextus,
    That wrought the deed of shame :
With restless pace and haggard face
    To his last field he came.
Men said he saw strange visions
    Which none beside might see ;

And that strange sounds were in his
    ears
    Which none might hear but he.
A woman fair and stately,
    But pale as are the dead,
Oft through the watches of the
    night
    Sat spinning by his bed.
And as she plied the distaff,
    In a sweet voice and low,
She sang of great old houses,
    And fights fought long ago.
So spun she, and so sang she,
    Until the east was grey,
Then pointed to her bleeding breast,
    And shrieked, and fled away.

XIII

But in the centre thickest
    Were ranged the shields of foes,
And from the centre loudest
    The cry of battle rose.
There Tibur marched and Pedum
    Beneath proud Tarquin's rule,
And Ferentinum of the rock,
    And Gabii of the pool.
There rode the Volscian succours :
    There, in a dark stern ring,
The Roman exiles gathered close
    Around the ancient king.
Though white as Mount Soracte,
    When winter nights are long,
His beard flowed down o'er mail and
        belt,
    His heart and hand were strong :

TARQUIN

Under his hoary eyebrows
  Still flashed forth quenchless rage :
And, if the lance shook in his gripe,
  'Twas more with hate than age.
Close at his side was Titus
  On an Apulian steed,
Titus, the youngest Tarquin,
  Too good for such a breed.

XIV

Now on each side the leaders
  Gave signal for the charge ;
And on each side the footmen
  Strode on with lance and targe ;
And on each side the horsemen
  Struck their spurs deep in gore,
And front to front the armies
  Met with a mighty roar :

And under that great battle
   The earth with blood was red ;
And, like the Pomptine fog at morn,
   The dust hung overhead ;
And louder still and louder
   Rose from the darkened field
The braying of the war-horns,
   The clang of sword and shield,
The rush of squadrons sweeping
   Like whirlwinds o'er the plain,
The shouting of the slayers,
   And screeching of the slain.

XV

False Sextus rode out foremost :
   His look was high and bold ;
His corslet was of bison's hide,
   Plated with steel and gold.

As glares the famished eagle
　　From the Digentian rock
On a choice lamb that bounds alone
　　Before Bandusia's flock,
Herminius glared on Sextus,
　　And came with eagle speed,
Herminius on black Auster,
　　Brave champion on brave steed ;
In his right hand the broadsword
　　That kept the bridge so well,
And on his helm the crown he won
　　When proud Fidenæ fell.
Woe to the maid whose lover
　　Shall cross his path to-day !
False Sextus saw, and trembled,
　　And turned, and fled away.
As turns, as flies, the woodman
　　In the Calabrian brake,

When through the reeds gleams the
    round eye
Of that fell speckled snake ;
So turned, so fled, false Sextus,
    And hid him in the rear,
Behind the dark Lavinian ranks,
    Bristling with crest and spear.

XVI

But far to north Æbutius,
    The Master of the Knights,
Gave Tubero of Norba
    To feed the Porcian kites.
Next under those red horse-hoofs
    Flaccus of Setia lay ;
Better had he been pruning
    Among his elms that day.
Mamilius saw the slaughter,
    And tossed his golden crest,

And towards the Master of the Knights
  Through the thick battle pressed.
Æbutius smote Mamilius
  So fiercely on the shield
That the great lord of Tusculum
  Well nigh rolled on the field.
Mamilius smote Æbutius,
  With a good aim and true,
Just where the neck and shoulder join,
  And pierced him through and through;
And brave Æbutius Elva
  Fell swooning to the ground :
But a thick wall of bucklers
  Encompassed him around.
His clients from the battle
  Bare him some little space,
And filled a helm from the dark lake,
  And bathed his brow and face ;

And when at last he opened
  His swimming eyes to light,
Men say, the earliest word he spake
  Was, " Friends, how goes the fight ? "

XVII

But meanwhile in the centre
  Great deeds of arms were wrought ;
There Aulus the Dictator
  And there Valerius fought.
Aulus with his good broadsword
  A bloody passage cleared
To where, amidst the thickest foes,
  He saw the long white beard.
Flat lighted that good broadsword
  Upon proud Tarquin's head.
He dropped the lance : he dropped the
    reins :
  He fell as fall the dead.

Down Aulus springs to slay him,
　　With eyes like coals of fire ;
But faster Titus hath sprung down,
　　And hath bestrode his sire.
Latian captains, Roman knights,
　　Fast down to earth they spring,
And hand to hand they fight on foot
　　Around the ancient king.
First Titus gave tall Cæso
　　A death wound in the face :
Tall Cæso was the bravest man
　　Of the brave Fabian race :
Aulus slew Rex of Gabii,
　　The priest of Juno's shrine :
Valerius smote down Julius,
　　Of Rome's great Julian line ;
Julius, who left his mansion
　　High on the Velian hill,

And through all turns of weal and woe
    Followed proud Tarquin still.
Now right across proud Tarquin
    A corpse was Julius laid ;
And Titus groaned with rage and grief,
    And at Valerius made.
Valerius struck at Titus,
    And lopped off half his crest ;
But Titus stabbed Valerius
    A span deep in the breast ;
Like a mast snapped by the tempest,
    Valerius reeled and fell.
Ah ! woe is me for the good house
    That loves the people well !
Then shouted loud the Latines ;
    And with one rush they bore
The struggling Romans backward
    Three lances' length and more :

And up they took proud Tarquin,
 And laid him on a shield,
And four strong yeomen bare him,
 Still senseless, from the field.

XVIII

But fiercer grew the fighting,
 Around Valerius dead ;
For Titus dragged him by the foot,
 And Aulus by the head.
" On, Latines, on ! " quoth Titus,
 " See how the rebels fly ! "
" Romans, stand firm ! " quoth Aulus,
 " And win this fight or die !
They must not give Valerius
 To raven and to kite ;
For aye Valerius loathed the wrong,
 And aye upheld the right :

5

And for your wives and babies
  In the front rank he fell.
Now play the men for the good house
  That loves the people well!"

XIX

Then tenfold round the body
  The roar of battle rose,
Like the roar of a burning forest,
  When a strong north wind blows.
Now backward, and now forward,
  Rocked furiously the fray,
Till none could see Valerius,
  And none wist where he lay.
For shivered arms and ensigns
  Were heaped there in a mound,
And corpses stiff, and dying men
  That writhed and gnawed the ground ;

And wounded horses kicking,
  And snorting purple foam :
Right well did such a couch befit
  A Consular of Rome.

XX

But north looked the Dictator ;
  North looked he long and hard ;
And spake to Caius Cossus,
  The Captain of his Guard ;
" Caius, of all the Romans
  Thou hast the keenest sight ;
Say, what through yonder storm of dust
  Comes from the Latian right ? "

XXI

Then answered Caius Cossus :
  " I see an evil sight ;

The banner of proud Tusculum
　　Comes from the Latian right ;
I see the plumed horsemen ;
　　And far before the rest
I see the dark-grey charger,
　　I see the purple vest ;
I see the golden helmet
　　That shines far off like flame ;
So ever rides Mamilius,
　　Prince of the Latian name."

XXII

" Now hearken, Caius Cossus :
　　Spring on thy horse's back ;
Ride as the wolves of Apennine
　　Were all upon thy track ;
Haste to our southward battle :
　　And never draw the rein

Until thou find Herminius,
  And bid him come amain."

XXIII

So Aulus spake, and turned him
  Again to that fierce strife ;
And Caius Cossus mounted,
  And rode for death and life.
Loud clanged beneath his horse-hoofs
  The helmets of the dead,
And many a curdling pool of blood
  Splashed him from heel to head.
So came he far to southward,
  Where fought the Roman host,
Against the banners of the marsh
  And banners of the coast.
Like corn before the sickle
  The stout Lavinians fell,

Beneath the edge of the true sword
That kept the bridge so well.

XXIV

" Herminius ! Aulus greets thee ;
He bids thee come with speed,
To help our central battle ;
For sore is there our need.
There wars the youngest Tarquin,
And there the Crest of Flame,
The Tusculan Mamilius,
Prince of the Latian name.
Valerius hath fallen fighting
In front of our array ;
And Aulus of the seventy fields
Alone upholds the day."

XXV

Herminius beat his bosom :
    But never a word he spake.
He clapped his hand on Auster's mane :
    He gave the reins a shake,
Away, away, went Auster,
    Like an arrow from the bow :
Black Auster was the fleetest steed
    From Aufidus to Po.

XXVI

Right glad were all the Romans
    Who, in that hour of dread,
Against great odds bare up the war
    Around Valerius dead,
When from the south the cheering
    Rose with a mighty swell ;
" Herminius comes, Herminius,
    Who kept the bridge so well ! "

XXVII

Mamilius spied Herminius,
　　And dashed across the way.
" Herminius ! I have sought thee
　　Through many a bloody day.
One of us two, Herminius,
　　Shall never more go home.
I will lay on for Tusculum,
　　And lay thou on for Rome ! "

XXVIII

All round them paused the battle,
　　While met in mortal fray
The Roman and the Tusculan,
　　The horses black and grey.
Herminius smote Mamilius
　　Through breast-plate and through
　　　breast,

And fast flowed out the purple blood
  Over the purple vest.
Mamilius smote Herminius
  Through head-piece and through head ;
And side by side those chiefs of pride
  Together fell down dead.
Down fell they dead together
  In a great lake of gore ;
And still stood all who saw them fall
  While men might count a score.

XXIX

Fast, fast, with heels wild spurning,
  The dark-grey charger fled :
He burst through ranks of fighting men ;
  He sprang o'er heaps of dead.
His bridle far out-streaming,
  His flanks all blood and foam,

He sought the southern mountains,
  The mountains of his home.
The pass was steep and rugged,
  The wolves they howled and whined ;
But he ran like a whirlwind up the pass,
  And he left the wolves behind.
Through many a startled hamlet
  Thundered his flying feet ;
He rushed through the gate of Tusculum,
  He rushed up the long white street ;
He rushed by tower and temple,
  And paused not from his race
Till he stood before his master's door
  In the stately market-place.
And straightway round him gathered
  A pale and trembling crowd,
And when they knew him, cries of rage
  Brake forth, and wailing loud :

And women rent their tresses
  For their great prince's fall ;
And old men girt on their old swords,
  And went to man the wall.

XXX

But, like a graven image,
  Black Auster kept his place,
And ever wistfully he looked
  Into his master's face.
The raven-mane that daily,
  With pats and fond caresses,
The young Herminia washed and combed,
  And twined in even tresses,
And decked with coloured ribands
  From her own gay attire,
Hung sadly o'er her father's corpse
  In carnage and in mire.

Forth with a shout sprang Titus,
   And seized black Auster's rein.
Then Aulus sware a fearful oath,
   And ran at him amain.
" The furies of thy brother
   With me and mine abide,
If one of your accursed house
   Upon black Auster ride ! "
As on an Alpine watch-tower
   From heaven comes down the flame,
Full on the neck of Titus
   The blade of Aulus came :
And out the red blood spouted,
   In a wide arch and tall,
As spouts a fountain in the court
   Of some rich Capuan's hall.
The knees of all the Latines
   Were loosened with dismay,

When dead, on dead Herminius,
    The bravest Tarquin lay.

XXXI

And Aulus the Dictator
    Stroked Auster's raven mane,
With heed he looked unto the girths,
    With heed unto the rein.
"Now bear me well, black Auster,
    Into yon thick array ;
And thou and I will have revenge
    For thy good lord this day."

XXXII

So spake he ; and was buckling
    Tighter black Auster's band,
When he was aware of a princely pair
    That rode at his right hand.

So like they were, no mortal
    Might one from other know:
White as snow their armour was:
    Their steeds were white as snow.
Never on earthly anvil
    Did such rare armour gleam;
And never did such gallant steeds
    Drink of an earthly stream.

XXXIII

And all who saw them trembled,
    And pale grew every cheek;
And Aulus the Dictator
    Scarce gathered voice to speak.
" Say by what name men call you?
    What city is your home?
And wherefore ride ye in such guise
    Before the ranks of Rome?"

XXXIV

" By many names men call us ;
  In many lands we dwell :
Well Samothracia knows us ;
  Cyrene knows us well.
Our house in gay Tarentum
  Is hung each morn with flowers :
High o'er the masts of Syracuse
  Our marble portal towers ;
But by the proud Eurotas
  Is our dear native home ;
And for the right we come to fight
  Before the ranks of Rome."

XXXV

So answered those strange horsemen,
  And each couched low his spear ;
And forthwith all the ranks of Rome
  Were bold, and of good cheer :

And on the thirty armies
　　Came wonder and affright,
And Ardea wavered on the left,
　　And Cora on the right.
" Rome to the charge ! " cried Aulus ;
　　" The foe begins to yield !
Charge for the hearth of Vesta !
　　Charge for the Golden Shield !
Let no man stop to plunder,
　　But slay, and slay, and slay ;
The Gods who live for ever
　　Are on our side to-day."

XXXVI

Then the fierce trumpet-flourish
　　From earth to heaven arose,
The kites know well the long stern swell
　　That bids the Romans close.

Then the good sword of Aulus
    Was lifted up to slay :
Then, like a crag down Apennine,
    Rushed Auster through the fray.
But under those strange horsemen
    Still thicker lay the slain ;
And after those strange horses
    Black Auster toiled in vain.
Behind them Rome's long battle
    Came rolling on the foe,
Ensigns dancing wild above,
    Blades all in line below.
So comes the Po in flood-time
    Upon the Celtic plain :
So comes the squall, blacker than night,
    Upon the Adrian main.
Now, by our Sire Quirinus,
    It was a goodly sight

6

To see the thirty standards
    Swept down the tide of flight.
So flies the spray of Adria
    When the black squall doth blow ;
So corn-sheaves in the flood-time
    Spin down the whirling Po.
False Sextus to the mountains
    Turned first his horse's head ;
And fast fled Ferentinum,
    And fast Lanuvium fled.
The horsemen of Nomentum
    Spurred hard out of the fray ;
The footmen of Velitræ
    Threw shield and spear away.
And underfoot was trampled,
    Amidst the mud and gore,
The banner of proud Tusculum,
    That never stooped before :

And down went Flavius Faustus,
   Who led his stately ranks
From where the apple blossoms wave
   On Anio's echoing banks,
And Tullus of Arpinum,
   Chief of the Volscian aids,
And Metius with the long fair curls,
   The love of Anxur's maids,
And the white head of Vulso,
   The great Arician seer,
And Nepos of Laurentum,
   The hunter of the deer ;
And in the back false Sextus
   Felt the good Roman steel,
And wriggling in the dust he died,
   Like a worm beneath the wheel :
And fliers and pursuers
   Were mingled in a mass ;

And far away the battle
　　Went roaring through the pass.

XXXVII

Sempronius Atratinus
　　Sate in the Eastern Gate,
Beside him were three Fathers,
　　Each in his chair of state ;
Fabius, whose nine stout grandsons
　　That day were in the field,
And Manlius, eldest of the twelve
　　Who keep the Golden Shield ;
And Sergius, the High Pontiff,
　　For wisdom far renowned ;
In all Etruria's colleges
　　Was no such Pontiff found.
And all around the portal,
　　And high above the wall,

Stood a great throng of people,
  But sad and silent all ;
Young lads, and stooping elders
  That might not bear the mail,
Matrons with lips that quivered,
  And maids with faces pale.
Since the first gleam of daylight,
  Sempronius had not ceased
To listen for the rushing
  Of horse-hoofs from the east.
The mist of eve was rising,
  The sun was hastening down,
When he was aware of a princely pair
  Fast pricking towards the town.
So like they were, man never
  Saw twins so like before ;
Red with gore their armour was,
  Their steeds were red with gore.

XXXVIII

" Hail to the great Asylum !
　　Hail to the Hill-tops seven !
Hail to the fire that burns for aye,
　　And the shield that fell from heaven !
This day, by Lake Regillus,
　　Under the Porcian height,
All in the lands of Tusculum
　　Was fought a glorious fight.
To-morrow your Dictator
　　Shall bring in triumph home
The spoils of thirty cities
　　To deck the shrines of Rome ! "

XXXIX

Then burst from that great concourse
　　A shout that shook the towers,
And some ran north, and some ran south,
　　Crying, " The day is ours ! "

But on rode these strange horsemen,
   With slow and lordly pace ;
And none who saw their bearing
   Durst ask their name or race.
On rode they to the Forum,
   While laurel-boughs and flowers,
From house-tops and from windows,
   Fell on their crests in showers.
When they drew nigh to Vesta,
   They vaulted down amain,
And washed their horses in the well
   That springs by Vesta's fane.
And straight again they mounted,
   And rode to Vesta's door ;
Then, like a blast, away they passed,
   And no man saw them more.

XL

And all the people trembled,
　　And pale grew every cheek ;
And Sergius the High Pontiff
　　Alone found voice to speak :
" The Gods who live for ever
　　Have fought for Rome to-day !
These be the Great Twin Brethren
　　To whom the Dorians pray.
Back comes the Chief in triumph,
　　Who, in the hour of fight,
Hath seen the Great Twin Brethren,
　　In harness on his right.
Safe comes the ship to haven,
　　Through billows and through gales,
If once the Great Twin Brethren
　　Sit shining on the sails.

Wherefore they washed their horses
 In Vesta's holy well,
Wherefore they rode to Vesta's door,
 I know, but may not tell.
Here, hard by Vesta's temple,
 Build we a stately dome
Unto the Great Twin Brethren
 Who fought so well for Rome.
And when the months returning
 Bring back this day of fight,
The proud Ides of Quintilis,
 Marked evermore with white,
Unto the Great Twin Brethren
 Let all the people throng,
With chaplets and with offerings,
 With music and with song ;
And let the doors and windows
 Be hung with garlands all,

And let the Knights be summoned
　To Mars without the wall :
Thence let them ride in purple
　With joyous trumpet-sound,
Each mounted on his war-horse,
　And each with olive crowned ;
And pass in solemn order
　Before the sacred dome,
Where dwell the Great Twin Brethren
　Who fought so well for Rome."

CASTOR   AND   POLLVX

VIRGINIA

FRAGMENTS OF A LAY SUNG IN THE FORUM
ON THE DAY WHEREON LUCIUS SEXTIUS
SEXTINUS LATERANUS AND CAIUS LICI-
NIUS CALVUS STOLO WERE ELECTED
TRIBUNES OF THE COMMONS THE FIFTH
TIME, IN THE YEAR OF THE CITY
CCCLXXXII

YE good men of the Commons, with
loving hearts and true,

Who stand by the bold Tribunes that
    still have stood by you,
Come, make a circle round me, and
    mark my tale with care,
A tale of what Rome once hath borne,
    of what Rome yet may bear.
This is no Grecian fable, of fountains
    running wine,
Of maids with snaky tresses, or sailors
    turned to swine.
Here, in this very Forum, under the
    noonday sun,
In sight of all the people, the bloody
    deed was done.
Old men still creep among us who saw
    that fearful day,
Just seventy years and seven ago, when
    the wicked Ten bare sway.

Of all the wicked Ten still the names
    are held accursed,
And of all the wicked Ten Appius
    Claudius was the worst.
He stalked along the Forum like King
    Tarquin in his pride :
Twelve axes waited on him, six marching
    on a side ;
The townsmen shrank to right and left,
    and eyed askance with fear
His lowering brow, his curling mouth
    which always seemed to sneer :
That brow of hate, that mouth of scorn,
    marks all the kindred still ;
For never was there Claudius yet but
    wished the Commons ill :
Nor lacks he fit attendance ; for close
    behind his heels,

With outstretched chin and crouching
    pace, the client Marcus steals,
His loins girt up to run with speed, be
    the errand what it may,
And the smile flickering on his cheek,
    for aught his lord may say.
Such varlets pimp and jest for hire among
    the lying Greeks :
Such varlets still are paid to hoot when
    brave Licinius speaks.
Where'er ye shed the honey, the buzzing
    flies will crowd ;
Where'er ye fling the carrion, the raven's
    croak is loud ;
Where'er down Tiber garbage floats, the
    greedy pike ye see ;
And wheresoe'er such lord is found, such
    client still will be.

Just then, as through one cloudless
    chink in a black stormy sky
Shines out the dewy morning-star, a fair
    young girl came by.
With her small tablets in her hand, and
    her satchel on her arm,
Home she went bounding from the school,
    nor dreamed of shame or harm ;
And past those dreaded axes she inno-
    cently ran,
With bright, frank brow that had not
    learned to blush at gaze of man ;
And up the Sacred Street she turned,
    and, as she danced along,
She warbled gaily to herself lines of the
    good old song,
How for a sport the princes came spurring
    from the camp,

And found Lucrece, combing the fleece,
    under the midnight lamp.
The maiden sang as sings the lark, when
    up he darts his flight;
From his nest in the green April corn,
    to meet the morning light,
And Appius heard her sweet young voice,
    and saw her sweet young face,
And loved her with the accursed love of
    his accursed race,
And all along the Forum, and up the
    Sacred Street,
His vulture eye pursued the trip of those
    small glancing feet.

.   .   .   .

Over the Alban mountains the light of
    morning broke;

From all the roofs of the Seven Hills
    curled the thin wreaths of smoke :
The city-gates were opened; the Forum
    all alive,
With buyers and with sellers was hum-
    ming like a hive :
Blithely on brass and timber the crafts-
    man's stroke was ringing,
And blithely o'er her panniers the market-
    girl was singing,
And blithely young Virginia came smiling
    from her home :
Ah ! woe for young Virginia, the sweetest
    maid in Rome !
With her small tablets in her hand, and
    her satchel on her arm,
Forth she went bounding to the school,
    nor dreamed of shame or harm.

She crossed the Forum shining with stalls
    in alleys gay,
And just had reached the very spot where-
    on I stand this day,
When up the varlet Marcus came ; not
    such as when erewhile
He crouched behind his patron's heels
    with the true client smile :
He came with lowering forehead, swollen
    features, and clenched fist,
And strode across Virginia's path, and
    caught her by the wrist.
Hard strove the frightened maiden, and
    screamed with look aghast ;
And at her scream from right and left the
    folk came running fast ;
The money-changer Crispus, with his thin
    silver hairs,

And Hanno from the stately booth glitter-
    ing with Punic wares,
And the strong smith Muræna, grasping
    a half-forged brand,
And Volero the flesher, his cleaver in his
    hand.
All came in wrath and wonder; for all
    knew that fair child ;
And, as she passed them twice a day, all
    kissed their hands and smiled ;
And the strong smith Muræna gave Marcus
    such a blow,
The caitiff reeled three paces back, and
    let the maiden go.
Yet glared he fiercely round him, and
    growled in harsh, fell tone,
" She's mine, and I will have her : I seek
    but for mine own :

She is my slave, born in my house, and
    stolen away and sold,
The year of the sore sickness, ere she was
    twelve hours old.
'Twas in the sad September, the month
    of wail and fright,
Two augurs were borne forth that morn ;
    the Consul died ere night.
I wait on Appius Claudius, I waited on
    his sire :
Let him who works the client wrong
    beware the patron's ire ! "

    So spake the varlet Marcus ; and dread
    and silence came
On all the people at the sound of the
    great Claudian name.

For then there was no Tribune to speak
    the word of might,
Which makes the rich man tremble, and
    guards the poor man's right.
There was no brave Licinius, no honest
    Sextius then ;
But all the city, in great fear, obeyed the
    wicked Ten.
Yet ere the varlet Marcus again might
    seize the maid,
Who clung tight to Muræna's skirt, and
    sobbed, and shrieked for aid,
Forth through the throng of gazers the
    young Icilius pressed,
And stamped his foot, and rent his gown,
    and smote upon his breast,
And sprang upon that column, by many
    a minstrel sung,

Whereon three mouldering helmets, three
    rusting swords, are hung,
And beckoned to the people, and in bold
    voice and clear
Poured thick and fast the burning words
    which tyrants quake to hear.

" Now, by your children's cradles, now
    by your fathers' graves,
Be men to-day, Quirites, or be for ever slaves!
For this did Servius give us laws ?   For
    this did Lucrece bleed ?
For this was the great vengeance wrought
    on Tarquin's evil seed ?
For this did those false sons make red the
    axes of their sire ?
For this did Scævola's right hand hiss in
    the Tuscan fire ?

Shall the vile fox-earth awe the race that
stormed the lion's den ?
Shall we, who could not brook one lord,
crouch to the wicked Ten ?
Oh for that ancient spirit which curbed
the Senate's will !
Oh for the tents which in old time
whitened the Sacred Hill !
In those brave days our fathers stood
firmly side by side ;
They faced the Marcian fury ; they tamed
the Fabian pride :
They drove the fiercest Quinctius an out-
cast forth from Rome ;
They sent the haughtiest Claudius with
shivered fasces home.
But what their care bequeathed us our
madness flung away :

All the ripe fruit of threescore years was
  blighted in a day.
Exult, ye proud Patricians! The hard-
  fought fight is o'er.
We strove for honours—'twas in vain:
  for freedom—'tis no more.
No crier to the polling summons the
  eager throng;
No Tribune breathes the word of might
  that guards the weak from wrong.
Our very hearts, that were so high, sink
  down beneath your will.
Riches, and lands, and power, and state—
  ye have them :—keep them still.
Still keep the holy fillets; still keep the
  purple gown,
The axes, and the curule chair, the car,
  and laurel crown :

Still press us for your cohorts, and, when
    the fight is done,
Still fill your garners from the soil which
    our good swords have won.
Still, like a spreading ulcer, which leech-
    craft may not cure,
Let your foul usance eat away the
    substance of the poor.
Still let your haggard debtors bear all
    their fathers bore;
Still let your dens of torment be noisome
    as of yore;
No fire when Tiber freezes; no air in
    dog-star heat;
And store of rods for free-born backs,
    and holes for free-born feet.
Heap heavier still the fetters; bar closer
    still the grate;

Patient as sheep we yield us up unto
  your cruel hate.
But, by the Shades beneath us, and by
  the Gods above,
Add not unto your cruel hate your yet
  more cruel love !
Have ye not graceful ladies, whose spot-
  less lineage springs
From Consuls, and High Pontiffs, and
  ancient Alban kings ?
Ladies, who deign not on our paths to
  set their tender feet,
Who from their cars look down with
  scorn upon the wondering street,
Who in Corinthian mirrors their own
  proud smiles behold,
And breathe of Capuan odours, and shine
  with Spanish gold ?

Then leave the poor Plebeian his single
tie to life——
The sweet, sweet love of daughter, of
sister, and of wife,
The gentle speech, the balm for all that
his vexed soul endures,
The kiss, in which he half forgets even
such a yoke as yours.
Still let the maiden's beauty swell the
father's breast with pride;
Still let the bridegroom's arms infold an
unpolluted bride.
Spare us the inexpiable wrong, the un-
utterable shame,
That turns the coward's heart to steel,
the sluggard's blood to flame,
Lest, when our latest hope is fled, ye
taste of our despair,

And learn by proof, in some wild hour,
    how much the wretched dare."

.   .   .   .

.   .   .   .

    Straightway Virginius led the maid a
    little space aside,
To where the reeking shambles stood,
    piled up with horn and hide,
Close to yon low dark archway, where,
    in a crimson flood,
Leaps down to the great sewer the gurg-
    ling stream of blood.
Hard by, a flesher on a block had laid
    his whittle down :
Virginius caught the whittle up, and hid
    it in his gown.
And then his eyes grew very dim, and
    his throat began to swell,

And in a hoarse, changed voice he spake,
    " Farewell, sweet child ! Farewell !
Oh ! how I loved my darling ! Though
    stern I sometimes be,
To thee, thou know'st, I was not so.
    Who could be so to thee ?
And how my darling loved me ! How
    glad she was to hear
My footsteps on the threshold when I
    came back last year !
And how she danced with pleasure to
    see my civic crown,
And took my sword, and hung it up,
    and brought me forth my gown !
Now, all those things are over—yes, all
    thy pretty ways,
Thy needlework, thy prattle, thy snatches
    of old lays ;

And none will grieve when I go forth,
    or smile when I return,
Or watch beside the old man's bed, or
    weep upon his urn.
The house that was the happiest within
    the Roman walls,
The house that envied not the wealth
    of Capua's marble halls,
Now, for the brightness of thy smile,
    must have eternal gloom,
And for the music of thy voice, the
    silence of the tomb.
The time is come. See how he points
    his eager hand this way !
See how his eyes gloat on thy grief, like
    a kite's upon the prey !
With all his wit, he little deems, that,
    spurned, betrayed, bereft,

Thy father hath in his despair one fearful
    refuge left.
He little deems that in this hand I clutch
    what still can save
Thy gentle youth from taunts and blows,
    the portion of the slave ;
Yea, and from nameless evil, that passeth
    taunt and blow—
Foul outrage which thou knowest not,
    which thou shalt never know.
Then clasp me round the neck once
    more, and give me one more kiss ;
And now, mine own dear little girl, there
    is no way but this."
With that he lifted high the steel, and
    smote her in the side,
And in her blood she sank to earth,
    and with one sob she died.

Then, for a little moment, all people
    held their breath ;
And through the crowded Forum was
    stillness as of death ;
And in another moment brake forth
    from one and all
A cry as if the Volscians were coming
    o'er the wall.
Some with averted faces shrieking fled
    home amain ;
Some ran to call a leech ; and some ran
    to lift the slain :
Some felt her lips and little wrist, if life
    might there be found ;
And some tore up their garments fast,
    and strove to stanch the wound.
In vain they ran, and felt, and stanched ;
    for never truer blow

VIRGINIUS

That good right arm had dealt in fight
    against a Volscian foe.

  When Appius Claudius saw that deed,
    he shuddered and sank down,
And hid his face some little space with
    the corner of his gown,
Till, with white lips and bloodshot eyes,
    Virginius tottered nigh,
And stood before the judgment-seat,
    and held the knife on high.
"Oh! dwellers in the nether gloom,
    avengers of the slain,
By this dear blood I cry to you, do right
    between us twain ;
And even as Appius Claudius hath dealt
    by me and mine,

8

Deal you by Appius Claudius and all the
    Claudian line ! ”
So spake the slayer of his child, and
    turned, and went his way ;
But first he cast one haggard glance to
    where the body lay,
And writhed, and groaned a fearful
    groan, and then, with steadfast
    feet,
Strode right across the market-place unto
    the Sacred Street.

Then up sprang Appius Claudius :
    “ Stop him ; alive or dead !
Ten thousand pounds of copper to the
    man who brings his head.”
He looked upon his clients ; but none
    would work his will.

He looked upon his lictors ; but they
    trembled, and stood still.
And, as Virginius through the press his
    way in silence cleft,
Ever the mighty multitude fell back to
    right and left.
And he hath passed in safety unto his
    woeful home,
And there ta'en horse to tell the camp
    what deeds are done in Rome.

  By this the flood of people was swollen
    from every side,
And streets and porches round were filled
    with that o'erflowing tide ;
And close around the body gathered a
    little train

Of them that were the nearest and dearest
    to the slain.
They brought a bier, and hung it with
    many a cypress crown,
And gently they uplifted her, and gently
    laid her down.
The face of Appius Claudius wore the
    Claudian scowl and sneer,
And in the Claudian note he cried,
    " What doth this rabble here ?
Have they no crafts to mind at home,
    that hitherward they stray ?
Ho ! lictors, clear the market-place, and
    fetch the corpse away ! "
The voice of grief and fury till then had
    not been loud ;
But a deep sullen murmur wandered
    among the crowd,

Like the moaning noise that goes before
    the whirlwind on the deep,
Or the growl of a fierce watch-dog but
    half-aroused from sleep.
But when the lictors at that word, tall
    yeomen all and strong,
Each with his axe and sheaf of twigs,
    went down into the throng,
Those old men say, who saw that day of
    sorrow and of sin,
That in the Roman Forum was never
    such a din.
The wailing, hooting, cursing, the howls
    of grief and hate,
Were heard beyond the Pincian Hill,
    beyond the Latin Gate.
But close around the body, where stood
    the little train

Of them that were the nearest and dearest
to the slain,
No cries were there, but teeth set fast,
low whispers and black frowns,
And breaking up of benches, and girding
up of gowns.
'Twas well the lictors might not pierce
to where the maiden lay,
Else surely had they been all twelve torn
limb from limb that day.
Right glad they were to struggle back
blood streaming from their heads,
With axes all in splinters, and raiment all
in shreds.
Then Appius Claudius gnawed his lip, and
the blood left his cheek ;
And thrice he beckoned with his hand,
and thrice he strove to speak ;

And thrice the tossing Forum set up a
    frightful yell ;
"See, see, thou dog! what thou hast done ;
    and hide thy shame in hell!
Thou that wouldst make our maidens
    slaves must first make slaves of men.
Tribunes! Hurrah for Tribunes! Down
    with the wicked Ten!"
And straightway, thick as hailstones, came
    whizzing through the air
Pebbles, and bricks, and potsherds, all
    round the curule chair :
And upon Appius Claudius great fear and
    trembling came ;
For never was a Claudius yet brave against
    aught but shame.
Though the great houses love us not, we
    own, to do them right,

That the great houses, all save one, have
    borne them well in fight.
Still Caius of Corioli, his triumphs and
    his wrongs,
His vengeance and his mercy, live in our
    camp-fire songs.
Beneath the yoke of Furius oft have
    Gaul and Tuscan bowed ;
And Rome may bear the pride of him
    of whom herself is proud.
But evermore a Claudius shrinks from a
    stricken field,
And changes colour like a maid at sight
    of sword and shield.
The Claudian triumphs all were won
    within the city towers ;
The Claudian yoke was never pressed on
    any necks but ours.

A Cossus, like a wild cat, springs ever at
    the face ;
A Fabius rushes like a boar against the
    shouting chase ;
But the vile Claudian litter, raging with
    currish spite,
Still yelps and snaps at those who run,
    still runs from those who smite.
So now 'twas seen of Appius. When
    stones began to fly,
He shook, and crouched, and wrung his
    hands, and smote upon his thigh.
" Kind clients, honest lictors, stand by
    me in this fray !
Must I be torn in pieces ? Home, home,
    the nearest way ! "
While yet he spake, and looked around
    with a bewildered stare,

Four sturdy lictors put their necks
    beneath the curule chair;
And fourscore clients on the left, and
    fourscore on the right,
Arrayed themselves with swords and
    staves, and loins girt up for fight.
But, though without or staff or sword,
    so furious was the throng,
That scarce the train with might and
    main could bring their lord along.
Twelve times the crowd made at him;
    five times they seized his gown:
Small chance was his to rise again, if
    once they got him down:
And sharper came the pelting; and ever-
    more the yell—
" Tribunes ! we will have Tribunes ! "—
    rose with a louder swell:

And the chair tossed as tosses a bark with
    tattered sail
When raves the Adriatic beneath an
    eastern gale,
When the Calabrian sea-marks are lost
    in clouds of spume,
And the great Thunder-Cape has donned
    his veil of inky gloom.
One stone hit Appius in the mouth, and
    one beneath the ear ;
And ere he reached Mount Palatine, he
    swooned with pain and fear.
His cursed head, that he was wont to
    hold so high with pride,
Now, like a drunken man's, hung down,
    and swayed from side to side ;
And when his stout retainers had brought
    him to his door,

His face and neck were all one cake of
  filth and clotted gore.
As Appius Claudius was that day, so may
  his grandson be !
God send Rome one such other sight,
  and send me there to see !

.   .   .   .

THE PROPHECY OF CAPYS

A LAY SUNG AT THE BANQUET IN THE
CAPITOL, ON THE DAY WHEREON
MANIUS CURIUS DENTATUS, A SECOND
TIME CONSUL, TRIUMPHED OVER KING
PYRRHUS AND THE TARENTINES, IN
THE YEAR OF THE CITY CCCCLXXIX

I

Now slain is King Amulius,
  Of the great Sylvian line,

Who reigned in Alba Longa,
On the throne of Aventine.
Slain is the Pontiff Camers,
Who spake the words of doom :
" The children to the Tiber,
The mother to the tomb."

II

In Alba's lake no fisher
His net to-day is flinging :
On the dark rind of Alba's oaks
To-day no axe is ringing :
The yoke hangs o'er the manger :
The scythe lies in the hay :
Through all the Alban villages
No work is done to-day.

III

And every Alban burgher
  Hath donned his whitest gown ;
And every head in Alba
  Weareth a poplar crown ;
And every Alban door-post
  With boughs and flowers is gay ;
For to-day the dead are living ;
  The lost are found to-day.

IV

They were doomed by a bloody king :
  They were doomed by a lying priest :
They were cast on the raging flood :
  They were tracked by the raging beast :
Raging beast and raging flood
  Alike have spared the prey ;
And to-day the dead are living :
  The lost are found to-day.

V

The troubled river knew them,
   And smoothed his yellow foam
And gently rocked the cradle
   That bore the fate of Rome.
The ravening she-wolf knew them,
   And licked them o'er and o'er,
And gave them of her own fierce milk,
   Rich with raw flesh and gore.
Twenty winters, twenty springs,
   Since then have rolled away ;
And to-day the dead are living :
   The lost are found to-day.

VI

Blithe it was to see the twins,
   Right goodly youths and tall,
Marching from Alba Longa
   To their old grandsire's hall.

Along their path fresh garlands
   Are hung from tree to tree :
Before them stride the pipers,
   Piping a note of glee.

VII

On the right goes Romulus,
   With arms to the elbows red,
And in his hand a broadsword,
   And on the blade a head—
A head in an iron helmet,
   With horse-hair hanging down,
A shaggy head, a swarthy head,
   Fixed in a ghastly frown—
The head of King Amulius
   Of the great Sylvian line,
Who reigned in Alba Longa,
   On the throne of Aventine.

9

VIII

On the left side goes Remus,
    With wrists and fingers red,
And in his hand a boar-spear,
    And on the point a head—
A wrinkled head and aged,
    With silver beard and hair,
And holy fillets round it,
    Such as the pontiffs wear—
The head of ancient Camers,
    Who spake the words of doom :
" The children to the Tiber ;
    The mother to the tomb."

IX

Two and two behind the twins
    Their trusty comrades go,
Four and forty valiant men,
    With club, and axe, and bow.

CAPYS

On each side every hamlet
Pours forth its joyous crowd,
Shouting lads and baying dogs,
And children laughing loud,
And old men weeping fondly
As Rhea's boys go by,
And maids who shriek to see the heads,
Yet, shrieking, press more nigh.

X

So they marched along the lake;
They marched by fold and stall,
By corn-field and by vineyard,
Unto the old man's hall.

XI

In the hall-gate sate Capys,
Capys, the sightless seer;

From head to foot he trembled
　　As Romulus drew near.
And up stood stiff his thin white hair,
　　And his blind eyes flashed fire :
"Hail! foster child of the wonderous nurse!
　　Hail ! son of the wonderous sire !

XII

" But thou—what dost thou here
　　In the old man's peaceful hall ?
What doth the eagle in the coop,
　　The bison in the stall ?
Our corn fills many a garner ;
　　Our vines clasp many a tree ;
Our flocks are white on many a hill ;
　　But these are not for thee.

XIII

" For thee no treasure ripens
　　In the Tartessian mine :

For thee no ship brings precious bales
   Across the Libyan brine :
Thou shalt not drink from amber ;
   Thou shalt not rest on down ;
Arabia shall not steep thy locks,
   Nor Sidon tinge thy gown.

XIV

" Leave gold and myrrh and jewels,
   Rich table and soft bed,
To them who of man's seed are born,
   Whom woman's milk have fed.
Thou wast not made for lucre,
   For pleasure, nor for rest ;
Thou, that art sprung from the War-god's
     loins,
And hast tugged at the she-wolf's breast.

XV

" From sunrise unto sunset
 All earth shall hear thy fame :
A glorious city thou shalt build,
 And name it by thy name :
And there, unquenched through ages,
 Like Vesta's sacred fire,
Shall live the spirit of thy nurse,
 The spirit of thy sire.

XVI

" The ox toils through the furrow,
 Obedient to the goad ;
The patient ass, up flinty paths,
 Plods with his weary load :
With whine and bound the spaniel
 His master's whistle hears ;
And the sheep yields her patiently
 To the loud clashing shears.

XVII

" But thy nurse will hear no master,
　Thy nurse will bear no load ;
And woe to them that shear her,
　And woe to them that goad !
When all the pack, loud baying,
　Her bloody lair surrounds,
She dies in silence, biting hard,
　Amidst the dying hounds.

XVIII

" Pomona loves the orchard ;
　And Liber loves the vine;
And Pales loves the straw-built shed
　Warm with the breath of kine ;
And Venus loves the whispers
　Of plighted youth and maid,
In April's ivory moonlight
　Beneath the chestnut shade.

XIX

" But thy father loves the clashing
  Of broadsword and of shield :
He loves to drink the steam that reeks
  From the fresh battle-field :
He smiles a smile more dreadful
  Than his own dreadful frown,
When he sees the thick black cloud of smoke
  Go up from the conquered town.

XX

" And such as is the War-god,
  The author of thy line,
And such as she who suckled thee,
  Even such be thou and thine.
Leave to the soft Campanian
  His baths and his perfumes ;
Leave to the sordid race of Tyre
  Their dyeing-vats and looms :

Leave to the sons of Carthage
 The rudder and the oar :
Leave to the Greek his marble Nymphs
 And scrolls of wordy lore.

XXI

" Thine, Roman, is the pilum :
 Roman, the sword is thine,
The even trench, the bristling mound,
 The legion's ordered line ;
And thine the wheels of triumph,
 Which with their laurelled train
Move slowly up the shouting streets
 To Jove's eternal fane.

XXII

" Beneath thy yoke the Volscian
 Shall vail his lofty brow :

Soft Capua's curled revellers
 Before thy chairs shall bow :
The Lucumoes of Arnus
 Shall quake thy rods to see ;
And the proud Samnite's heart of steel
 Shall yield to only thee.

XXIII

" The Gaul shall come against thee
 From the land of snow and night :
Thou shalt give his fair-haired armies
 To the raven and the kite.

XXIV

" The Greek shall come against thee,
 The conqueror of the East.
Beside him stalks to battle
 The huge earth-shaking beast,

The beast on whom the castle
   With all its guards doth stand,
The beast who hath between his eyes
   The serpent for a hand.
First march the bold Epirotes,
   Wedged close with shield and spear;
And the ranks of false Tarentum
   Are glittering in the rear.

XXV

" The ranks of false Tarentum
   Like hunted sheep shall fly :
In vain the bold Epirotes
   Shall round their standards die :
And Apennine's grey vultures
   Shall have a noble feast
On the fat and the eyes
   Of the huge earth-shaking beast.

XXVI

" Hurrah ! for the good weapons
    That keep the War-god's land.
Hurrah ! for Rome's stout pilum
    In a stout Roman hand.
Hurrah ! for Rome's short broadsword,
    That through the thick array
Of levelled spears and serried shields
    Hews deep its gory way.

XXVII

" Hurrah ! for the great triumph
    That stretches many a mile.
Hurrah ! for the wan captives
    That pass in endless file.
Ho ! bold Epirotes, whither
    Hath the Red King ta'en flight ?
Ho ! dogs of false Tarentum,
    Is not the gown washed white ?

XXVIII

" Hurrah ! for the great triumph
   That stretches many a mile.
Hurrah ! for the rich dye of Tyre,
   And the fine web of Nile,
The helmets gay with plumage
   Torn from the pheasant's wings,
The belts set thick with starry gems
   That shone on Indian kings,
The urns of massy silver,
   The goblets rough with gold,
The many-coloured tablets bright
   With loves and wars of old,
The stone that breathes and struggles,
   The brass that seems to speak ;—
Such cunning they who dwell on high
   Have given unto the Greek.

XXIX

" Hurrah ! for Manius Curius,
  The bravest son of Rome,
Thrice in utmost need sent forth,
  Thrice drawn in triumph home.
Weave, weave, for Manius Curius
  The third embroidered gown :
Make ready the third lofty car,
  And twine the third green crown ;
And yoke the steeds of Rosea
  With necks like a bended bow ;
And deck the bull, Mevania's bull,
  The bull as white as snow.

XXX

" Blest and thrice blest the Roman
  Who sees Rome's brightest day,
Who sees that long victorious pomp
Wind down the Sacred Way,

And through the bellowing Forum,
   And round the Suppliant's Grove,
Up to the everlasting gates
   Of Capitolian Jove.

XXXI

" Then where, o'er two bright havens,
   The towers of Corinth frown ;
Where the gigantic King of Day
   On his own Rhodes looks down ;
Where soft Orontes murmurs
   Beneath the laurel shades ;
Where Nile reflects the endless length
   Of dark-red colonnades ;
Where in the still deep water,
   Sheltered from waves and blasts,
Bristles the dusky forest
   Of Byrsa's thousand masts ;

Where fur-clad hunters wander
  Amidst the northern ice ;
Where through the sand of morning-land
  The camel bears the spice ;
Where Atlas flings his shadow
  Far o'er the western foam,
Shall be great fear on all who hear
  The mighty name of Rome."

PRINTED BY NEILL AND CO., LTD., EDINBURGH.